Composer's Choice

ABOUT THE SERIES

The Composer's Choice series showcases piano works by an exclusive group of composers. Each collection contains classic piano pieces that were carefully chosen by the composer, as well as brand-new pieces written especially for the series. Helpful performance notes are also included.

ISBN 978-1-5400-4582-9

WILLIS MUSIC

EXCLUSIVELY DISTRIBUTED BY

HAL•LEONARD®

Visit Hal Leonard Online at
www.halleonard.com

Contact us:
Hal Leonard
7777 West Bluemound Road
Milwaukee, WI 53213
Email: info@halleonard.com

In Europe, contact:
Hal Leonard Europe Limited
42 Wigmore Street
Marylebone, London, W1U 2RN
Email: info@halleonardeurope.com

In Australia, contact:
Hal Leonard Australia Pty. Ltd.
4 Lentara Court
Cheltenham, Victoria, 3192 Australia
Email: info@halleonard.com.au

FROM THE COMPOSER

This collection contains six of my favorite pieces and two new compositions. There's variety! I've chosen a couple of pieces that have a traditional Japanese sound; another depicts heartfelt emotion. Two duets were transformed into solo arrangements.

When I create music, I often begin with the melody. The process of adding harmonies and rhythms to the melody is enjoyable to me. I like to think that it is similar to adding strokes to a painting, scenes to a movie, or plot twists to a novel.

Listening to performances of my works brings me great pleasure. I find the different sound colors in each performance wonderful because it takes broad imagination to enrich the black and white music on these pages.

I want *you* to become the hero or heroine of these eight musical stories. Enjoy!

Naoko Ikeda

Sapporo, July 2019

CONTENTS

PERFORMANCE NOTES

BY NAOKO IKEDA

SOFT RAIN

"Soft Rain" is from *Miyabi*, a collection of pieces that feature a distinct Japanese sound. The rainy season in June is called *tsuyu*. The hydrangeas (*azisai*) are particularly beautiful—and peaceful—after the rain. You will hear Japanese traditional scales in the melody mixed in with modern harmonies. Play with a graceful, delicate touch.

...YOU

This piece is from *Shoukei*, my very first collection. It is one of my most popular pieces in Japan! I wanted the melody and harmony to be reminiscent of an American pop ballade from the 1980s. The 16th notes should be played as if speaking to someone very special. Choose a word that comes before "you" in the title.

SAKURA

Like "...You," this piece is from *Shoukei* (Book 1). *Sakura* (cherry blossoms) symbolize the Japanese spring. Imagine floating flower petals and play expressively. In measure 25 imitate these flower petals fluttering in the breeze. The triplet in measure 27 should be played gently.

THE GLACIAL MERMAID

This is the solo version of a piece from my first duet collection, "Winter Songs." The setting is a faraway land of ice and snow. It's early in the afternoon and there's a soft, beautiful voice in the distance. It's coming from the statue of a mermaid in the park. She's singing for her dream that she will swim in a real sea someday. The second beat of measure 18 is a glistening of ice as it melts a little in the sun. The left hand in measure 27 is the motion of imaginary waves.

LAND OF THE MIDNIGHT SUN

This piece is from the collection *Aurora*, inspired by the landscapes of Northern Europe. I have not experienced the *aurora borealis* (yet), but I find images of this elegant phenomena inspiring, majestic, and amazing. Arpeggiations should be unhurried, with the melody creating a mystical mood.

SCARLET HEARTS

This is a brand-new solo version of the piece from Book 1 of *Duets in Color*, my collection of duets in 12 major and minor keys. As such, the ballade features melodies sung by two voices in different ranges, tenor and alto. (I hope you play and experience the duet version as well!) In measure 18 play the 16th notes lightly, and be aware of the harmonic structure of the moving bass notes.

SHOOTING STARS IN SUMMER

> A night of shooting stars
> Seen from different sides of distant shores
> In time insight dawns;
> No promises are broken.
>
> A night of shooting stars
> Enveloping the colossal universe
> And love sings blissful dreams
> From which it never wakes.

In 2015 I was thrilled when "Shooting Stars in Summer" was selected to be on the repertoire list for The Royal Conservatory. The piece is from the collection *Celestial Dreams*, a book about the night skies above us. I chose the key of A Major because of its clear and open tone. Practice each phrase carefully and let the melody sing. For more efficient practice, work out the best fingering for the left hand. The triplets symbolize the wonder of shooting stars, and the next time you see one, I hope you make a special wish!

ARIGATO

Arigato is perhaps the Japanese word most understood outside Japan. It expresses one's gratitude. I think it is a kind, thoughtful, and powerful word in any language. I wrote this piece with a vocalise in mind, so play the melody expressively, as if you are physically singing. Note that the role of the accompaniment in the left hand changes subtly and often assists in moving the music forward. The first four notes of the piece sing *A-ri-ga-to*.

Soft Rain
(Azisai)

Naoko Ikeda

azisai = hydrangeas

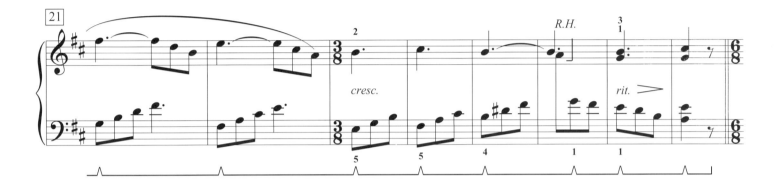

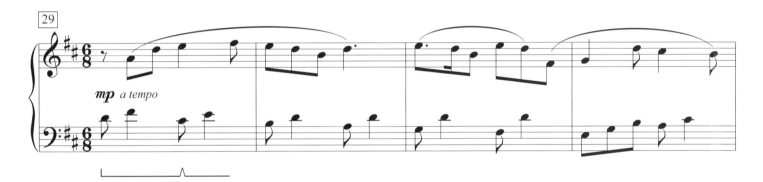

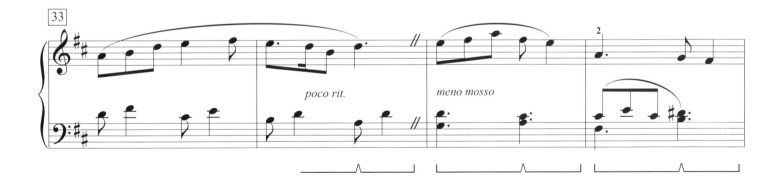

...You

Naoko Ikeda

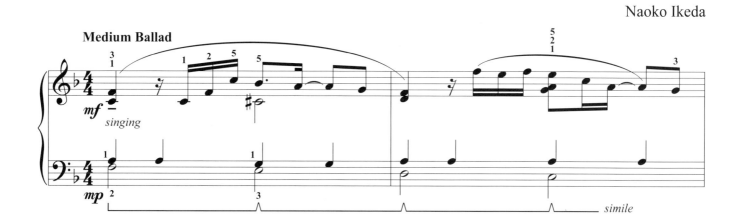

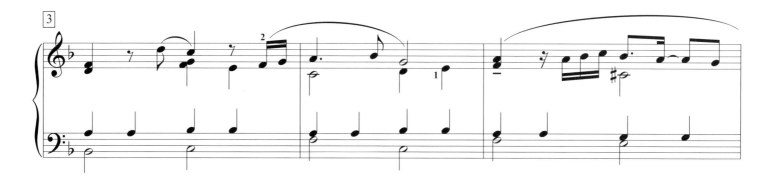

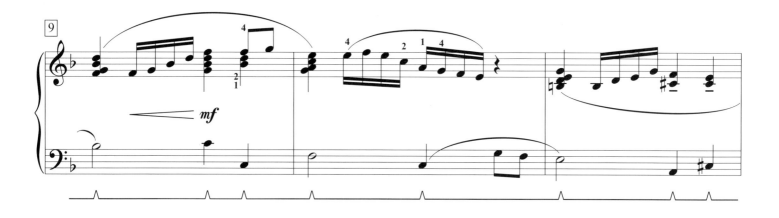

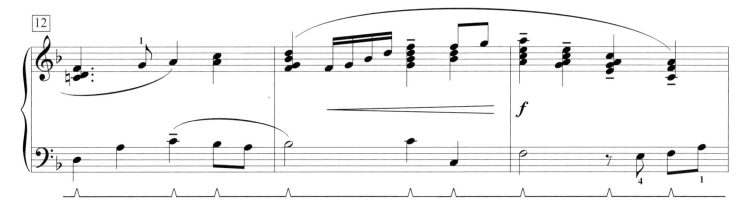

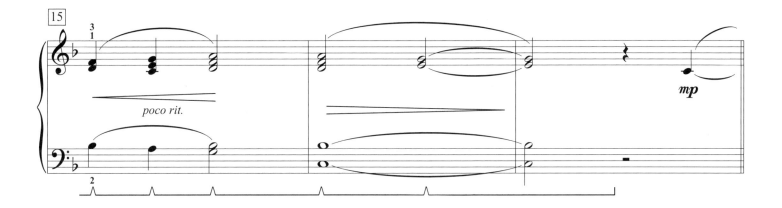

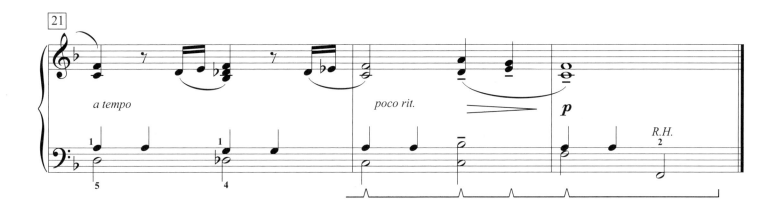

Sakura

Naoko Ikeda

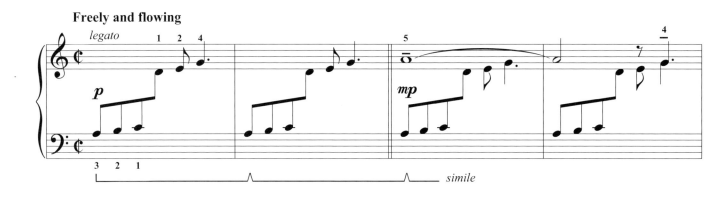

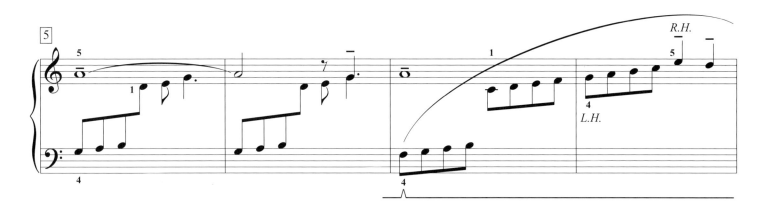

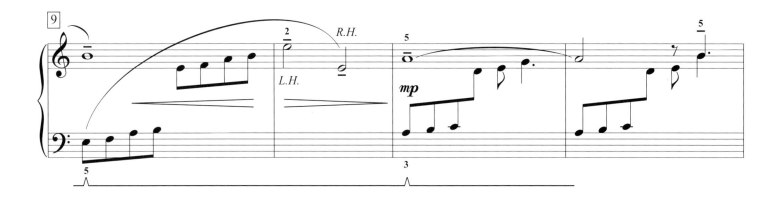

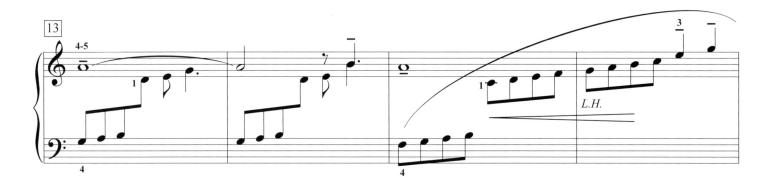

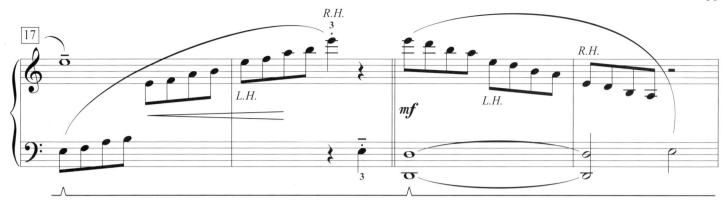

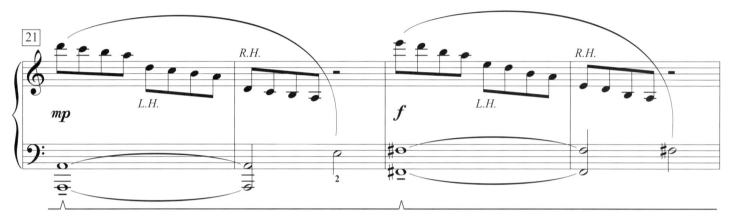

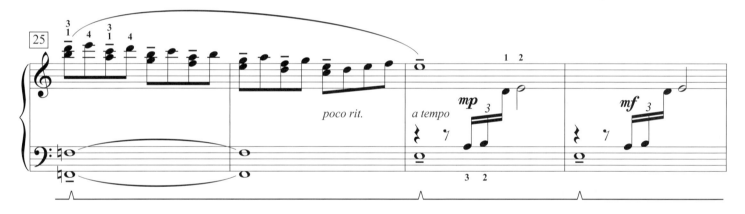

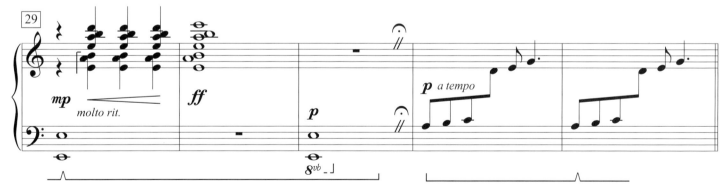

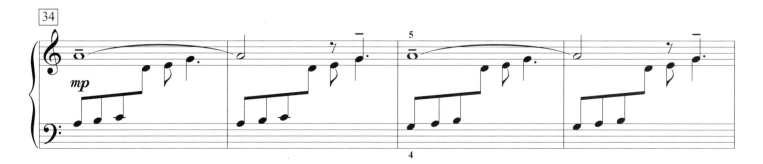

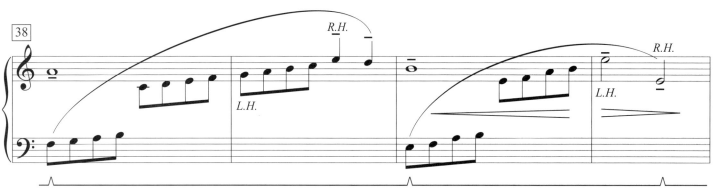

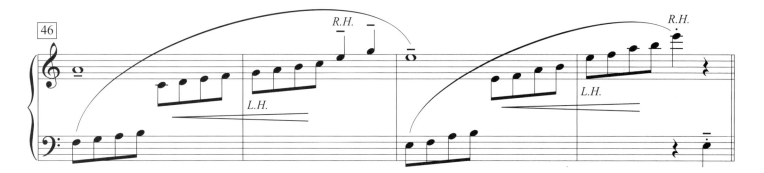

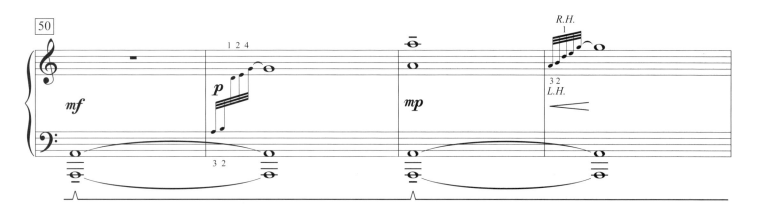

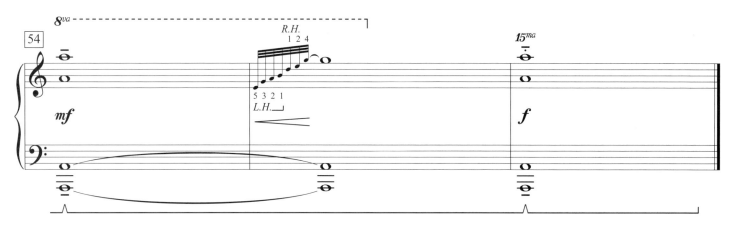

The Glacial Mermaid

Naoko Ikeda

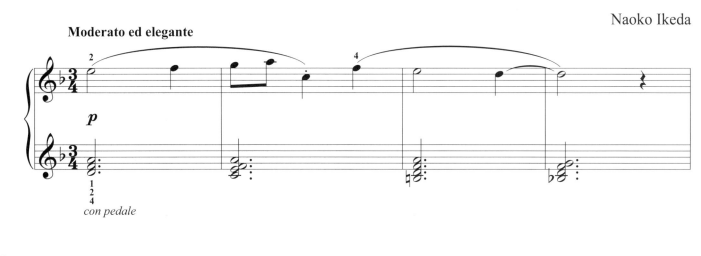

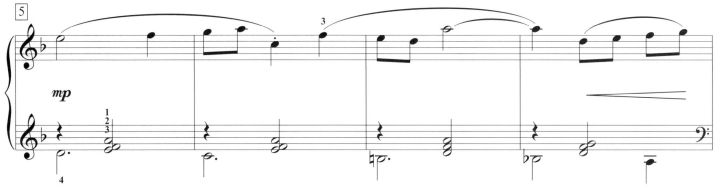

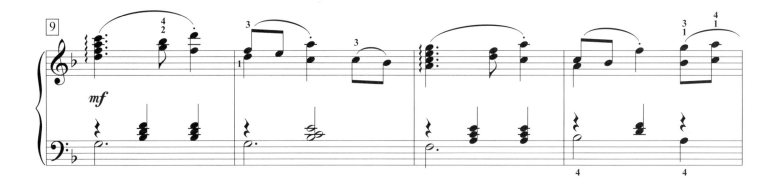

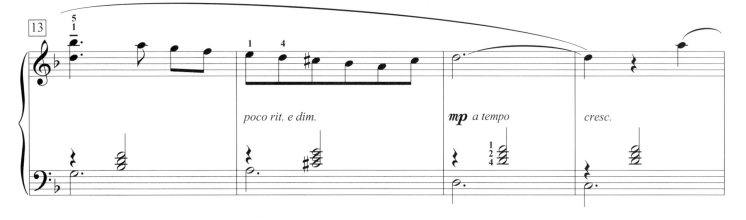

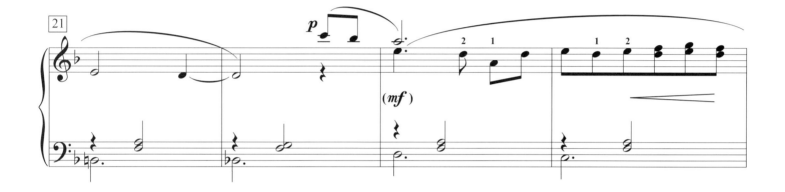

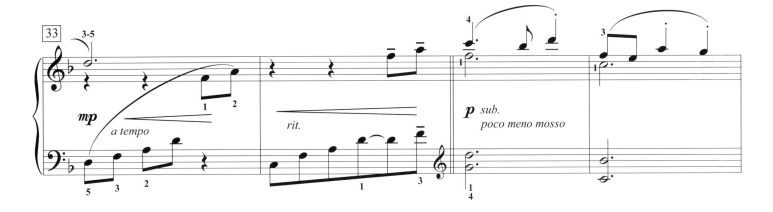

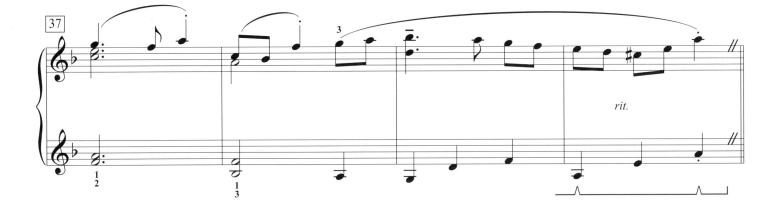

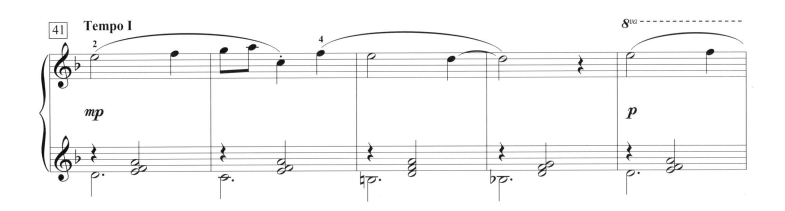

Land of the Midnight Sun

Naoko Ikeda

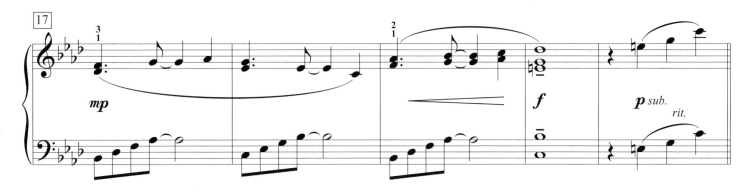

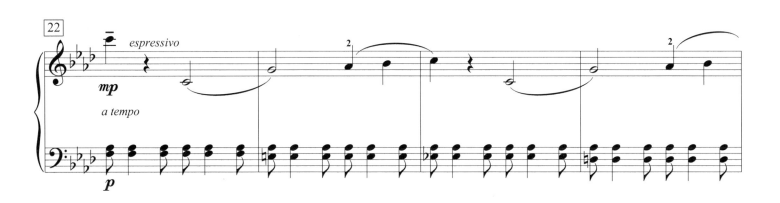

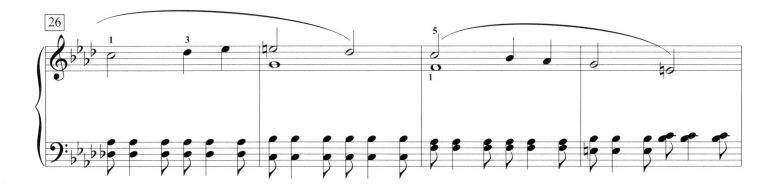

poco rit. e dim.

p a tempo

mp

cresc.

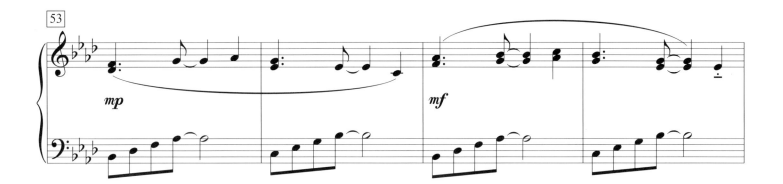

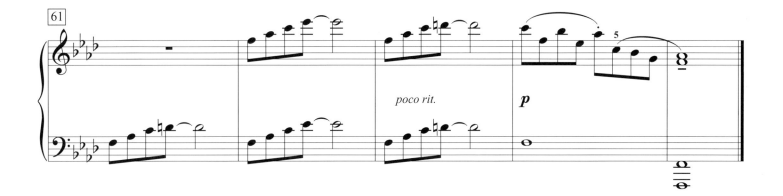

Scarlet Hearts

Naoko Ikeda

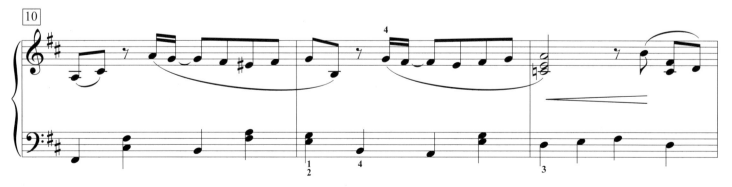

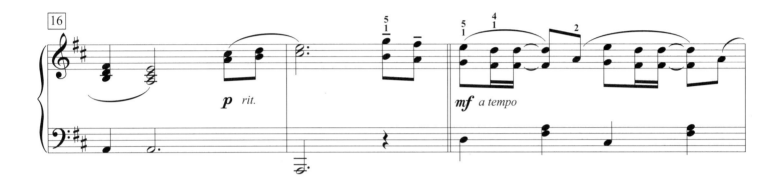

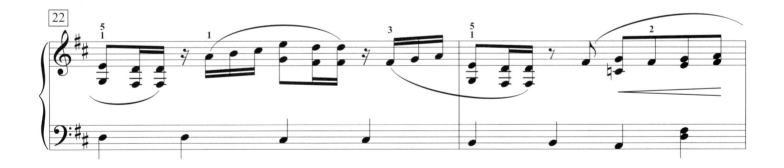

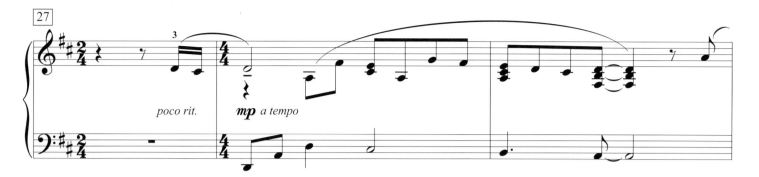

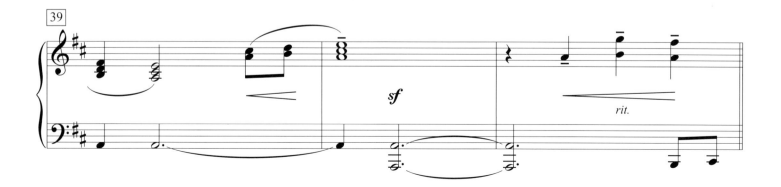

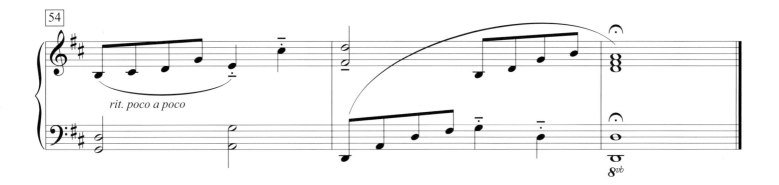

Shooting Stars in Summer

Naoko Ikeda

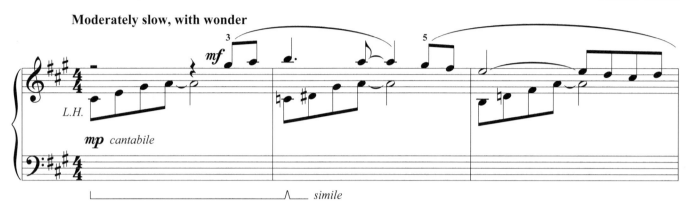

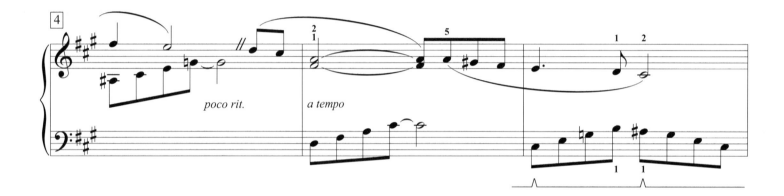

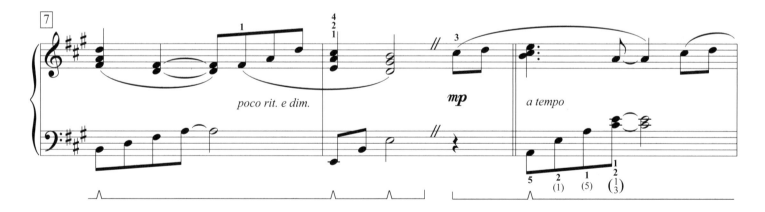

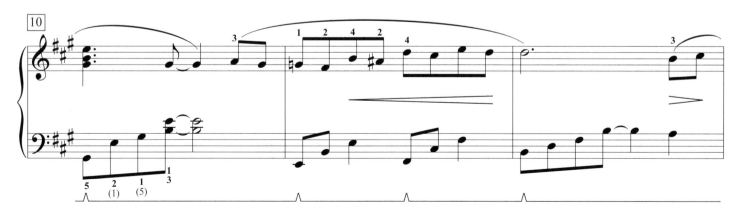

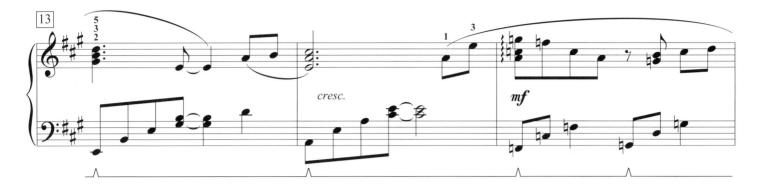

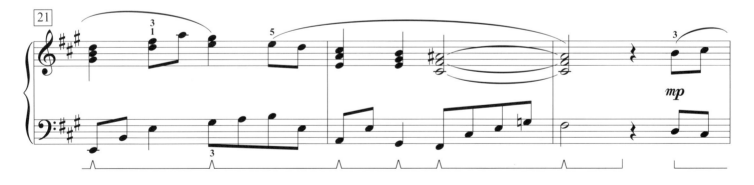

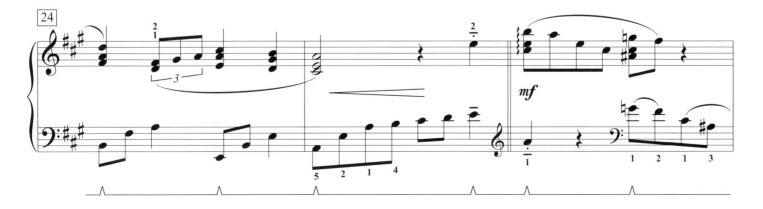

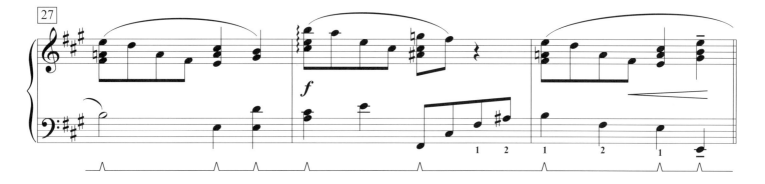

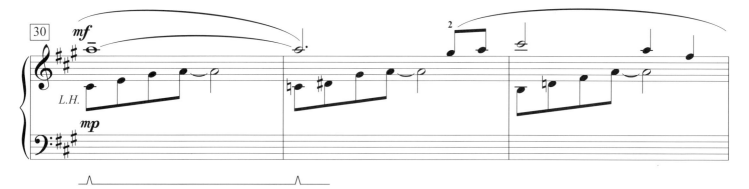

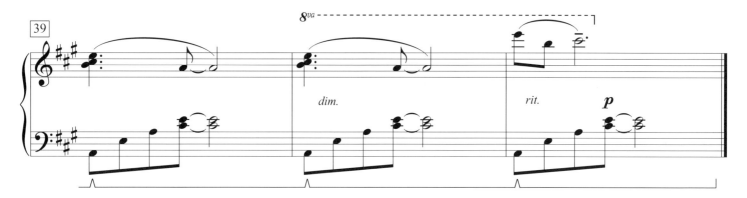

Arigato

With my deepest gratitude

Naoko Ikeda

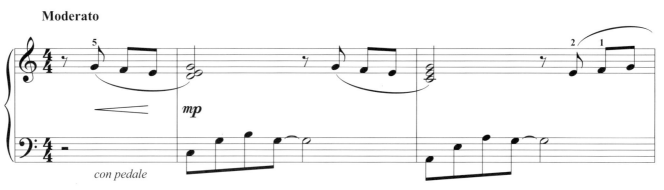

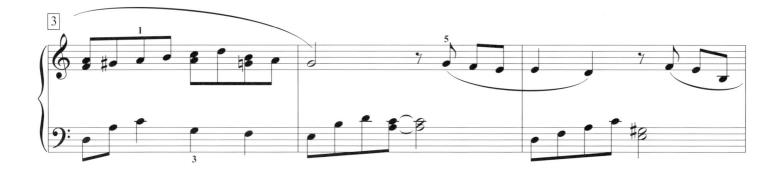

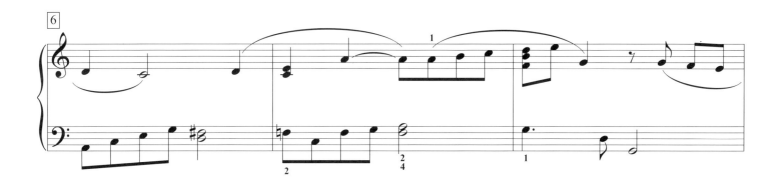

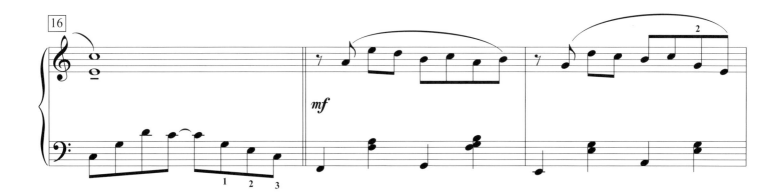

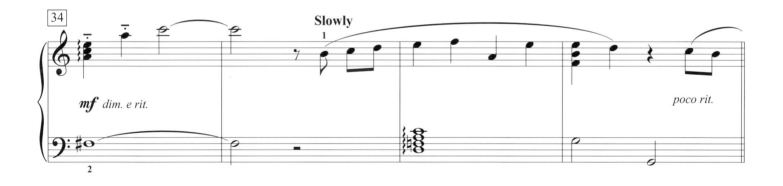

CLASSIC PIANO REPERTOIRE

The *Classic Piano Repertoire* series includes popular as well as lesser-known pieces from a select group of composers out of the Willis piano archives. Every piece has been newly engraved and edited with the aim to preserve each composer's original intent and musical purpose.

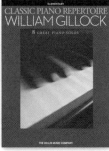

WILLIAM GILLOCK – ELEMENTARY

8 Great Piano Solos

Dance in Ancient Style • Little Flower Girl of Paris • On a Paris Boulevard • Rocking Chair Blues • Sliding in the Snow • Spooky Footsteps • A Stately Sarabande • Stormy Weather.

00416957 ....$8.99

EDNA MAE BURNAM – ELEMENTARY

8 Great Piano Solos

The Clock That Stopped • The Friendly Spider • A Haunted House • New Shoes • The Ride of Paul Revere • The Singing Cello • The Singing Mermaid • Two Birds in a Tree.

00110228 ....$8.99

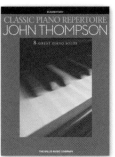

JOHN THOMPSON – ELEMENTARY

9 Great Piano Solos

Captain Kidd • Drowsy Moon • Dutch Dance • Forest Dawn • Humoresque • Southern Shuffle • Tiptoe • Toy Ships • Up in the Air.

00111968 ....$8.99

LYNN FREEMAN OLSON – EARLY TO LATER ELEMENTARY

14 Great Piano Solos

Caravan • Carillon • Come Out! Come Out! (Wherever You Are) • Halloween Dance • Johnny, Get Your Hair Cut! • Jumping the Hurdles • Monkey on a Stick • Peter the Pumpkin Eater • Pony Running Free • Silent Shadows • The Sunshine Song • Tall Pagoda • Tubas and Trumpets • Winter's Chocolatier.

00294722 ....$9.99

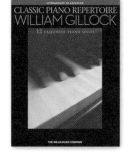

WILLIAM GILLOCK – INTERMEDIATE TO ADVANCED

12 Exquisite Piano Solos

Classic Carnival • Etude in A Major (The Coral Sea) • Etude in E Minor • Etude in G Major (Toboggan Ride) • Festive Piece • A Memory of Vienna • Nocturne • Polynesian Nocturne • Sonatina in Classic Style • Sonatine • Sunset • Valse Etude.

00416912 .... $12.99

EDNA MAE BURNAM – INTERMEDIATE TO ADVANCED

13 Memorable Piano Solos

Butterfly Time • Echoes of Gypsies • Hawaiian Leis • Jubilee! • Longing for Scotland • Lovely Senorita • The Mighty Amazon River • Rumbling Rumba • The Singing Fountain • Song of the Prairie • Storm in the Night • Tempo Tarantelle • The White Cliffs of Dover.

00110229 .... $12.99

JOHN THOMPSON – INTERMEDIATE TO ADVANCED

12 Masterful Piano Solos

Andantino (from Concerto in D Minor) • The Coquette • The Faun • The Juggler • Lagoon • Lofty Peaks • Nocturne • Rhapsody Hongroise • Scherzando in G Major • Tango Carioca • Valse Burlesque • Valse Chromatique.

00111969 .... $12.99

LYNN FREEMAN OLSON – EARLY TO MID-INTERMEDIATE

13 Distinctive Piano Solos

Band Wagon • Brazilian Holiday • Cloud Paintings • Fanfare • The Flying Ship • Heroic Event • In 1492 • Italian Street Singer • Mexican Serenade • Pageant Dance • Rather Blue • Theme and Variations • Whirlwind.

00294720 ....$9.99

WILLIS MUSIC

CLOSER LOOK View sample pages and hear audio excerpts online at www.halleonard.com

www.willispianomusic.com

www.facebook.com/willispianomusic

Prices, content, and availability subject to change without notice.

The Composer's Choice series showcases piano works by an exclusive group of composers, all of whom are also teachers and performers. Each collection contains 8 original solos and includes classic piano pieces that were carefully chosen by the composer, as well as brand-new compositions written especially for the series. The composers also contributed helpful and valuable performance notes for each collection. Get to know a new Willis composer today!

CLOSER LOOK

View sample pages and hear audio excerpts online at
www.halleonard.com

f @WillisPianoMusic

🔘 willispiano

🐦 @WillisPiano

▶ Willis Piano Music

ELEMENTARY

GLENDA AUSTIN
MID TO LATER ELEMENTARY
Betcha-Can Boogie • Jivin' Around • The Plucky Penguin • Rolling Clouds • Shadow Tag • Southpaw Swing • Sunset Over the Sea • Tarantella (Spider at Midnight).
00130168 ....$6.99

CAROLYN MILLER
MID TO LATER ELEMENTARY
The Goldfish Pool • March of the Gnomes • More Fireflies • Morning Dew • Ping Pong • The Piper's Dance • Razz-a-ma-tazz • Rolling River.
00118951 ....$7.99

CAROLYN C. SETLIFF
EARLY TO LATER ELEMENTARY
Dark and Stormy Night • Dreamland • Fantastic Fingers • Peanut Brittle • Six Silly Geese • Snickerdoodle • Roses in Twilight • Seahorse Serenade.
00119289 ....$7.99

EXCLUSIVELY DISTRIBUTED BY

HAL•LEONARD®

www.willispianomusic.com

Prices, contents, and availability subject to change without notice.

INTERMEDIATE

GLENDA AUSTIN
EARLY TO MID-INTERMEDIATE
Blue Mood Waltz • Chromatic Conversation • Etude in E Major • Midnight Caravan • Reverie • South Sea Lullaby • Tangorific • Valse Belle.
00115242 ....$9.99

ERIC BAUMGARTNER
EARLY TO MID-INTERMEDIATE
Aretta's Rhumba • Beale Street Boogie • The Cuckoo • Goblin Dance • Jackrabbit Ramble • Journey's End • New Orleans Nocturne • Scherzando.
00114465 ....$9.99

RANDALL HARTSELL
EARLY TO MID-INTERMEDIATE
Above the Clouds • Autumn Reverie • Raiders in the Night • River Dance • Showers at Daybreak • Sunbursts in the Rain • Sunset in Madrid • Tides of Tahiti.
00122211 ....$8.99

NAOKO IKEDA
EARLY TO MID-INTERMEDIATE
Arigato • The Glacial Mermaid • Land of the Midnight Sun • Sakura • Scarlet Hearts (solo version) • Shooting Stars in Summer • Soft Rain (Azisai) • ...You.
00288891 ....$8.99

CAROLYN MILLER
EARLY INTERMEDIATE
Allison's Song • Little Waltz in E Minor • Reflections • Ripples in the Water • Arpeggio Waltz • Trumpet in the Night • Toccata Semplice • Rhapsody in A Minor.
00123897 ....$8.99

CLASSICAL PIANO SOLOS
Original Keyboard Pieces from Baroque to the 20th Century

Compiled and edited by Philip Low, Sonya Schumann, and Charmaine Siagian

First Grade

22 pieces: *Bartók*: A Conversation • *Mélanie Bonis*: Miaou! Ronron! • *Burgmüller*: Arabesque • *Handel*: Passepied • *d'Indy*: Two-Finger Partita • *Köhler*: Andantino • *Müller*: Lyric Etude • *Ryba*: Little Invention • *Schytte*: Choral Etude; Springtime • *Türk*: I Feel So Sick and Faint, and more!

00119738 / $6.99

Second Grade

22 pieces: *Bartók*: The Dancing Pig Farmer • *Beethoven*: Ecossaise • *Bonis*: Madrigal • *Burgmüller*: Progress • *Gurlitt*: Etude in C • *Haydn*: Dance in G • *d'Indy*: Three-Finger Partita • *Kirnberger*: Lullaby in F • *Mozart*: Minuet in C • *Petzold*: Minuet in G • *Purcell*: Air in D Minor • *Rebikov*: Limping Witch Lurking • *Schumann*: Little Piece • *Schytte*: A Broken Heart, and more!

00119739 / $6.99

Third Grade

20 pieces: *CPE Bach*: Presto in C Minor • *Bach/Siloti*: Prelude in G • *Burgmüller*: Ballade • *Cécile Chaminade*: Pièce Romantique • *Dandrieu*: The Fifers • *Gurlitt*: Scherzo in D Minor • *Hook*: Rondo in F • *Krieger*: Fantasia in C • *Kullak*: Once Upon a Time • *MacDowell*: Alla Tarantella • *Mozart*: Rondino in D • *Rebikov*: Playing Soldiers • *Scarlatti*: Sonata in G • *Schubert*: Waltz in F Minor, and more!

00119740 / $7.99

Fourth Grade

18 pieces: *CPE Bach*: Scherzo in G • *Teresa Carreño*: Berceuse • *Chopin*: Prelude in E Minor • *Gade*: Little Girls' Dance • *Granados*: Valse Poetic No. 6 • *Grieg*: Arietta • *Handel*: Prelude in G • *Heller*: Sailor's Song • *Kuhlau*: Sonatina in C • *Kullak*: Ghost in the Fireplace • *Moszkowski*: Tarentelle • *Mozart*: Allegro in G Minor • *Rebikov*: Music Lesson • *Satie*: Gymnopedie No. 1 • *Scarlatti*: Sonata in G • *Telemann*: Fantasie in C, and more!

00119741 / $7.99

Fifth Grade

19 pieces: *Bach*: Prelude in C-sharp Major • *Beethoven:* Moonlight sonata • *Chopin*: Waltz in A-flat • *Cimarosa*: Sonata in E-flat • *Coleridge-Taylo*r: They Will Not Lend Me a Child • *Debussy*: Doctor Gradus • *Grieg*: Troldtog • *Griffes*: Lake at Evening • *Lyadov*: Prelude in B Minor • *Mozart*: Fantasie in D Minor • *Rachmaninoff*: Prelude in C-sharp Minor • *Rameau*: Les niais de Sologne • *Schumann:* Farewell • *Scriabin*: Prelude in D, and more!

00119742 / $8.99

The *Classical Piano Solos* series offers carefully-leveled, original piano works from Baroque to the early 20th century, featuring the simplest classics in Grade 1 to concert-hall repertoire in Grade 5. An assortment of pieces are featured, including familiar masterpieces by Bach, Beethoven, Mozart, Grieg, Schumann, and Bartók, as well as several lesser-known works by composers such as Melanie Bonis, Anatoly Lyadov, Enrique Granados, Vincent d'Indy, Theodor Kullak, and Samuel Coleridge-Taylor.

- Grades 1-4 are presented in a suggested order of study. Grade 5 is laid out chronologically.

- Features clean, easy-to-read engravings with clear but minimal editorial markings.

- View complete repertoire lists of each book along with sample music pages at **www.willispianomusic.com**.

The series was compiled to loosely correlate with the *John Thompson Modern Course*, but can be used with any method or teaching situation.